FULL Fledged!

Be a step Ahead of a Narcissist!
No better revenge than Success!

A Must-Read!

AWARD WINNING!

Written By :

DeAnne Michelle Rhynehardt-Bousso

Contents

Acknowledgments

Introduction

Chapter 1

First you have to fail

Recognizing Narcissistic behaviors

Chapter 2

Through another person's eyes

Chapter 3

The Awakening of your authentic self,

Chapter 4

Focusing on you, rebuilding your future, and getting rid of the pain.

Chapter 5

Begin Self-training, clarity, and understanding why you were chosen.

Chapter 6

The Fight Back

Deciding to live your life pain-free and with no more setbacks.

Chapter 7

The definition of Full Fledged!

Building your own fortune

Acknowledgments

I would like to thank a few people in this book first being my mother, Pricilla Ann Rhynehardt who is my rock.

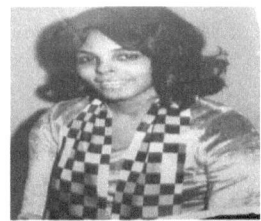 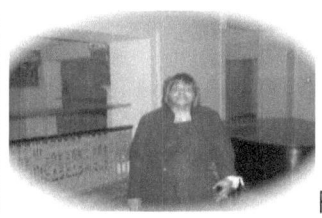

Pricilla Ann

My kids Antonio, Jermaine, Michelle Rhynehardt, & Charles Hickerson, Nephew /son Christopher Rhynehardt are the reason why I do what I do. Teresa Donette Foster, Lushunys (Shonnie) Rhynehardt, Anthony Rhynehardt, Sonja Rhynehardt, Junior Foster Aric Foster, Traci Smith, Yolanda Foster, Tiffany Hancock, Darren Long, Toni Long, Elton Campbell, Jeffrey Campbell Katrina Richardson.

Grand Children: Corrie Rhynehardt, Natalie Stewart-Rhynehardt, Kiko Keyshawn Rhynehardt- Jayde Rhynehardt, Jermaine (Maino) Rhynehardt Jr. Tyona Hickerson, Tyon Hickerson, Charles Hickerson Jr., God Daughter, Shamaine Richardson Mack, And Renea Pitts.

Auntie- Julia Campbell-Johnson Auntie, Deborah Wall & Michael Wall, Paula Gail Bester&George Bester, Sis Mable

Williams, Sis McNeal, Lavenia Neal, Sis Peoples, My Mothers best friends, *It takes a village* Terry Brown, Sis Green, Sis Moore, Sis Fountain, Alice Fountain, Pastor I.R. Witcher, Pastor & first lady Kemper

Ascc Direct.

These people really helped me through the video to give a better understanding as to what happened to me. I also want to acknowledge Brian Khanga for being an exact definition of a friend.

My friends and extended family:

Alena Hinkle, Angela Rhea, Tina O'Brien-Taylor, Kim Stubblefield, Athena Woodford, May May, Bridgette Willams Princess Smith, , Kirsis and Quasi Thomas, May Malyn, Mia Terry, Tamara Walker BRITTS LLC, William Walker, Phyllis Bowman (MY Favorite) Kish, Spanky, Snoop, Moo Moo,(I got you). Chris, and Bill Martha, Uncle William. Melani Church-Coleman & Marty Coleman, Glenda Smith, Mario, Daniel Johnson, Torres Shumpert-Stoudemire, Marcia Woods, Lavetra Winfrey,(Monica, Jessica, Timothy) Michelle & Stan Rogers, David Wilson Traci Wilson, William Wilson, Robin Bester- Wilson, , Denise Bester, Stephanie Bester, Curtis Cblow lol, Lisa Combs, Michael Clark, Ronald Lowe, Torres , Davon Washington, Michelle Rogers, Sabrina Johnson, Tracy Milligan, Kelley & Jimmy Foreman!

To anyone I missed who supported my book, my business or me through such a traumatic state, Thank you.

This book represents strength the everlasting determination to win.

In life you will have many challenges and people that want to destroy you, this will allow you to know, When you are in tune with God the ability to fight will be nothing short of impossible.

Allow this book to be a guide to men and women to help you see the truth in others and to help prevent you from getting hurt. Let my book be a source for you to have a pain free prosperous future! Real success comes to you once you have yourself and once you realize happiness is within. Knowing yourself makes you confident and happy within.

Chapter 1

The Beginning

This Book is not about my life and is told through another person eyes.

I am starting this book with the pain because it is how I found myself & success; it is how I found God.

To begin, my life has changed, my heart is different, my goals are different, my sight is different, I live in Romans 8 28-30.

"I believe God has called me. I speak differently, I hear him differently, I want to cry just texting this. I am stronger nothing can hurt me worldly; I live and have my being through Christ who strengthens me."

I can do nothing without him THIS I KNOW, in a way that I never knew, through my pain he came to me, my pain was a gift to secure my life with him so that I can serve and love him, with my whole heart, without a doubt...

I have been reborn through his grace, I am so humble and thankful because, HE DIDN"T HAVE TO DO IT!

Let me talk to you through the eyes of another, this book is to expose the many ways your dreams and your life can be set back also redirected. I am going to speak on Narcissism pretty heavy to begin because most of us are dealing with one or may even be one, whatever the case it needs to be addressed.

The purpose of pointing these characteristics are to bring you to focus, analyze you present life, to create a more focused you.

Relationships can be set backs if you choose someone that can't handle your potential or your growth.

A Narcissist can't reveal themselves right away; they are liars and very cunning, they have to be the victim to be right. They are afraid to be themselves because they first do not believe in themselves also they hate who they are, as they should.

Make no mistake narcissist can be your very best friend; your husband could be your worst enemy. My commitment was a huge set- back for me, bringing women in my house, and then accusing me of hurting him. As I reflect I will never forget the day a family member sending me a text saying "we both failed everyone." I wanted say "forget you" I didn't fail anyone, all of you failed me; with your fake ass love and deceitful lifestyles.

Love was the foundation of the committed and the termination of it as well. It takes a Narc to raise a Narc. Family defending lies "shame on you" I believe parental abused is real, It's takes a lot to know as a woman you have to take something so horrible to your grave, something so heinous as, another woman sleeping with your husband in your bed. Ones thoughts are, would you recover from the painful devastating event. How could a man do that to a woman? How could a female be so disrespectful and be okay with herself? How could a woman disregard the wife and not even care that he was sleeping with other women as well. In this moment, feelings are one feels like, surely God has forsaken me.

When this happens to a person, the feelings are ok is he trying to destroyed my soul, the tears are different. The pain takes your breath away. Staying busy was the goal looking back is not an option because it will destroy whatever is left. Something like this is not a normal break up this is the kind of break up that feels like you have been robbed. This is the type of deceit that felt criminal. Feels like you have been more than raped; in fact it is rape in many ways. If you were married, and fell in love with someone who never loved you intentionally, used and deceived you for whatever reason then discarded you like trash, well that is more than rape it is a kidnapping on another level.

This type of deceit makes you evaluate your whole life and your surroundings; you begin to calculate your every move. This type of deceit awakens the deepest senses of awareness.

This does not always happen with couple it can also happen with friends, please know this, when you agree to sleep with a man that has a woman/wife whatever the case, and you your- self are married, you are not with a Narc you are the Narc, and to be full-fledged in God you know this is not offensive to say, you know this is growth.

Playing the victim as they all do will not change this reality. One can't love you until they have shown remorse about their sins, as a friend or spouse they are not good for you and separate yourself.

It took everything in me just to get up in the mornings. God will use these type events to wake you up to eliminate, everything fake in your life. I don't judge I just tell the truth.

God took all the mess out my life. These kind people are indeed Narcs, they are watching your every move. Their families only know the surface of who they really are.

My mind is unique as is everyone's is, you can copy and you can even come up on the steal, but you can only be yourself.

Be yourself in everything you do and God will bless it. God let me know half of my friends were enemies especially the closest ones to me.

My encounter with a narcissist allowed me to be full-fledged in God. As I reflect I look at how I was lied to as he was capturing me, I was his prey, it was a game but better yet I was unaware of the game. My commitment was spat on with deceit and cheating. Everything we ever did, the very place he proposed to me he took another woman bought her the same gift and told her he loved her, and we were still committed not even a year. Prior to committing, we lived together my fiancé at the time, he was seeing a female maybe even more than one but this one, she even came to the wedding and continued seeing him after the marriage seeing him and receiving gifts. Explaining these details is important so that you can see these individuals, for who they really are, and eliminate them from your lives, and you can begin to stop lying to yourself.

Your soul is tainted for life after something like this happens to you.

These type individuals never genuinely wish you well, they will wish well, but inside they hope you fail.

I remember looking at both my friend and my husband I remember the look in their eyes, the look was envy, jealousy, and hate from my friend and from husband it was envy hate, jealousy, hate of me and my accomplishments, and also their own self-hate.

If you ask them how they are doing they always say things GREAT, or BLESSED, always appearing to the public to be happy and positive. On the flip side of the positive they go to the other extreme to make you believe their lies. For example: when Narcs get sick they act like they are deathly ill, like they might be dying, another example, their past relationships, everyone hurt them they never take ownership for their role, they are always the victim. These are text book NARCS!

Getting to know Narcissism-

To know if you are dealing with a covert narcissist, you must first understand what a covert narcissist is and that it comes in many forms and not just a man. Narcissist never owns anything and they know everything. Before I go any further please note I am not a Doctor or Psychologist nor am I saying this is my life experiences; I am merely a person conveying the truth from the experiences of another and through someone else's eyes.

Covert Narcissist:

The exact definition of a covert narcissist is this; covert narcissist, they "feel and "want "one way "believe" or "act" the opposite.

They have a false sense of reality, for example, they create characters that they want to be through their victims. So a covert narcissist is fully aware of what they are doing even when its wrong however while doing these things the Narc thinks they are right until when the mask is removed, so if they see qualities in you that help the character. These individuals want you to become then you are the chosen one. The covert narcissist will become whatever that characters needs him/her to be to get what they want, even if it means they have to marry you. You are nothing more than a piece of the puzzle nothing more. Loving you is not a part of the make-up even though they tell you they love you. A covert narcissist could very readily tell you, he/she loves you on the first date. You could be anyone; there is nothing special about you.

Characteristics of a Narcissists is essential for you to understand, Covert narcissist only love themselves; they are hard to detect because they are very cunning, and they adapt to whatever situation that is going on. Once the narcissist has got you under his wing and under his or her spell now it's time to find another source because they are now bored with you, so they begin to make mistakes now things like cheating lying stealing they may also begin to talk disrespectfully to you, they have no respect for you at all, at this stage. They may even sleep with a friend, or even in the home you shared.

Covert narcissist usually hurt the people the closest to them, and they have no remorse. They believe they are the victims so once the mask has been removed from their horrible, vile mess. They blame you for everything wrong going on in their life.

      A narcissist does not know what they want as it pertains to love and life as a whole. An example of a Narcissistic playground is the internet because this is an unlimited source and they can hide behind many characters; they have to be in control. Make no mistake the things they do are nothing short of horrible and in some cases even criminal. For example, my covert narcissist gave me a false birthdate; his birthday is actually May 16, 1965. However, no one knows this not even his job.

The covert narcissist is so smart that they know just when to draw the line so that when they are caught, you are left in such disarray you may even fire back which makes you look like you have been the abuser and he/she are the victim.

This is why this book is so important.

A covert narcissist is the worst in my opinion because they are they have no **remorse** once they have capsized your life. (key point)

Once you have dealt with a narcissist unless you understand what has happened to you, you will fall for another one.

(TRUTH)

I remember taking what I thought was a friend out to dinner and celebrating what I thought was success.

I even told her not to down play victories only to find out that she had lied about the victories which in turned pissed me off because in that moment I realized she was lying to intimidate me, it was a game and the enjoyment came through the possibility that it may have affected me in a negative way.

The feeling of being pissed and hurt was an understatement. After that day I could not be as open with my friends anymore I knew that those days were over and honestly we shouldn't anyway.

A Narc can and will act as though they dislike everything you like but they really want it for this for them; or they really love it, but they would never say this to you.

My narcissist told me he hated the car I chose, and he hated the color for example after we were over he went and bought a car the same color inside and out, because he really love the car I had, and most likely was jealous.

Narcissists are usually jealous, competitive, and selfish. Narcissist do not want to feel the feelings of embarrassment or shame they have no sense of loyalty they do not operate out of loyalty this is why they are they have no problem cheating, meaning anything goes when they are looking for them since of gratification.

Cheating is a breach of contract, and you should be upset, and you deserve Retribution, not an Apology.

The narcissist will cheat, and if you are with one, they ARE cheating, You have to know and accept they are incapable of being fully committed; they are always looking for something better than you. The grass is always better on the other side for them.

They do not know how to process people's good deeds, so in the end you always end up abused, hurt, and devastated.

The narcissist does not acknowledge commitment, but they make you believe they do. Narcissists are attention whores; they are always looking for attention which is why they cheat.

Narcs live through a false identity that they have created through you. (My narc love those Jason Borne movies) HA HA,

They are almost like a machine they continuously repeat the same reaction and interactions with different people, over and over again, producing the same results they do not attempt to change, adjust or correct the behavior or beliefs.

In relationships in the beginnings it easy to fall without knowing something is wrong with the picture, you feel loved better than you ever have been loved in your life, then over time you find yourself doing everything trying to please them and they are not doing anything to please you.

Most narcissists covert repeat the same cycle over and over again nothing changes other than the people in the situation and or relationships. It is sad and unfortunate when you think about it.

These individuals learn who you are to lure you in, once they learn this, they are determined to conquer you and in most cases, they will. When they are buying you gifts taking you on trips, love bombing you never wants to be without you just know this is not normal behavior of a healthy relationship. This is a trap know this recognize these characteristics.

Covert Narcissists are the worst of the narcissist by far because they are desperate and hard to detect because they usually hurt you to your core and discard you with no remorse. Please be aware.

Narcissist and silent treatment go hand in hand, this is very common with these individuals, the silent treatment is a way of control, and also a way of discarding you.

The silent treatment is a form of anger and control.

For example:

you may need the narcissist to give you a credit card that only he has access to purchase food for the house he will not answer the phone or answer text, or even come home thus holding the entire house from getting the food or access to something he/she agreed so freely within the beginning of the relationship.

These tactics are used to punish or control people.

This is very hurtful and gives you a feeling of rejection which is precisely how the narcissists feel always.

They take pleasure in your pain. Reasoning with these types of individuals is impossible, because they don't even see you as a person they see you as an object, this is why the can do such heinous things, such have sex with someone in the bed you share or taking someone on a date where he proposed to you.

Another example:

If you have a friend that dresses great at his/her events and then comes to your event in a ball cap wearing clothes you don't wear outside of the house, is hate in its truest form, the trickery is in the fact they showed up. So instead of you focusing on how they arrived, you appreciate the fact they came, it's a game.

Narcs never confront their feelings so when they are unmasked, they find a way to blame you and they become the victim. You only exist to them to be of service that is all.

Please know this!

When they leave you they hope you suffer and never recover; they also get joy out of seeing your pain and knowing this has happened to you.

When Narcissists has ghosted someone, they are not playing, and they are not coming back they are saying that you do not matter and they will not return. The intention is not to hurt or control or even punish the intention behind ghosting is to erase the other person do not confuse this with the silent treatment.

Emotional manipulation is very painful and is a real characteristic of a narcissist it is abuse. Protecting yourself from a narcissist is to set boundaries, make sure you know who you are and know what you want, do not stray from these standards and/or boundaries.

You can trust again if you have boundaries. If you give up on life and say things like "I will never love again" I will never whatever "

You allow the narcissist to win; I struggled in this area and still do. This is what he/she wants you to do they want to place death of failure upon your life after them.

Make no mistake you were seduced by this individual if something like this is happening in your life. At this point of life you have to learn your weaknesses and set your boundaries, Awareness is the goal of this book.

My goal is to expose the truth so that it does not happen to you! Helping you discover boundaries and helping you identify these individuals such as we discussed, in this book will also help you focus on you, and get on to the success that God has for your life. Narcissism is something that has always been around but most did not connect a name to it.

(Becoming Full Fledged)

To read a book such as this it means you are an in a full-fledged state, or it means that you are finding yourself for sure. It is a beautiful thing to find oneself.

To be in this place of reckoning, there are a few things that would have had to happen to you; above that, you are ready to live authentically.

(Being mentally present while reading this book is necessary because you are getting more acquainted with yourself.

　　While reading this book, I want you to get familiar with your values, skills, and your real interest. Who are you at the core of your soul? Start understanding your vision and your purpose.

I am trying to promote understanding challenging experiences through this story, also to provide clarity through my pain, strength and my success.)

(GETTING TO KNOW YOURSELF)

Knowing yourself is to know God in my opinion; I forgive the people intentionally hurt me, because knowing something more significant than oneself is the beginning of knowing who you are.

Getting to know yourself involves separating yourself from everything that you believe is real. You have to separate yourself from the noise.

When you are getting to know yourself THIS MEANS you and God are becoming one indeed.

When trying to find myself, I was a somewhat of a spiritual predator so to speak.

I knew it had to be something greater than me that was in control. Until life breaks you, you are a slave to yourself. During the process of evolution, you are not becoming self-absorbed, but you are being somewhat selfish during this process.

Narcissisms is a key factor in this book because most people are dealing with one in your life and don't know it so this book focuses on this to awaken your senses.

At this point of the book, jot down some notes looking into your own life. Do you see signs of Narcissistic behaviors in someone close to you? Does this person make major decisions in your life? Is this a friend, co-worker, husband, wife?

Be aware of your life!

Make Notes:

Chapter 2

"The truth will set you free, but first it will piss you off."

Understanding pain is good for you!

Through someone else's eyes

My late forties when I met what I thought was the love of my life. He asks me out on a date, and I was not really ready, and I felt he was begging for my time which made me suspicious. The first date was lunch as opposed to dinner, which was my idea, I wore the most unattractive outfit so to turn him off, it didn't work, so after the date he walked me to my car and he basically made sure he kissed me, however during this moment he hugged me and it was the tightest squeeze I had felt in a long time.

I loved the way he held me at that moment. Even though his hug was great, but I was not sold. We also talked on the phone for months before the first date, I felt pretty safe. During the time we were conversing on the phone he talked about me needing a new phone so on our first date he bought me a new phone. I felt weird even taking it also his **eyes** gave me this weird feeling almost like I was a piece of meat.

Mentioning the fact his **eyes** gave me a weird feeling, to my kids, they felt like maybe I was being overprotective that maybe he was a good guy and to give him a chance. After that, he bought four new tires on my car and then within a month telling me he loved me.

I felt like this has to be the best guy I have ever dated. He wanted to meet my parents and kids so after a few weeks of the same consistent treatment.

I allowed him to meet my family he also wanted to meet my friends as well. Within a year of getting together, we were married. All my friends celebrated him and he would publically profess his love to me online and also to anyone that we encountered.

Discarding any weird feelings I had of him because he treated me like I was a queen. The feeling I was having when all of this was going on was is this real? Have I really met someone that loves me unconditionally as he says?

This made me feel like I was indebted to him. All of these events happened in less than a year which made me feel like he was going to take care of me no matter what! He even told me if you do not want to work you do not have to.

    This all sounds ridiculous when reading it now even for me as I write this book, but as you are in it, you feel celebrated, loved and completely happy just as he wanted me to feel, If he had given me much time to think about it, he knew he may have lost me.

    My personality is very cordial and loving. I have respect for others, and I care about others without thought this is how I was raised. He was literally invisible no one knew he even existed. However, everyone loved, and I always received lots of what I like to think is positive attention from people and still do because I genuinely care about my friends and family and interact with heartfelt joy even when I am having a bad day.

So this is something I think he wanted from me, I believe he wanted to be noticed, he wanted to be popular, he wanted to feel like the man, and he wanted to use me to get that feeling. I was his new source of narcissistic supply.

    I meant absolutely nothing to him; my presence was merely the vehicle to be noticed. He enjoyed deceiving me and getting away with it. He enjoyed hurting me and watching me justify why he did what he did and that everything would be ok, he enjoy watching me be in pain.

    During our two year commitment, the first was bliss to me we traveled and bought things together; we lived really well. Things began to get stressful to him because as I stated before he wanted full control of the finances and bills, so he put me on his accounts. My paycheck every two weeks went to his account.

I began to feel comfortable, I felt like this is real and he did everything he said he was going to do. Feeling safe was present and I thanked him for being in my life. He wrote his own special words of commitment, and in his words, he stated that he would give me nothing short of the rest of his life and that he would be faithful, it was a breathtaking speech. About one year into the commitment my guard came down because he made me feel so safe.

The dynamics were changing, He seemed to enjoy my family they were always helping him, and my family loved and looked up to him. I was selling real estate along with my full-time job so at this point, with his encouragement, I decided to take on a greater role in the Industry and open my own company.

I finally felt safe, as a woman safety is a virtue, this man made me feel like a queen like there was nothing he would not do for me not only did he express this to me but he expressed it publically to anyone that we encountered. I felt wow finally I have met the man of my dreams. He is the one!

(Inside Story)

Our evenings were like this: we both worked 8 -10 hours a day on most occasions he would work more because he was in competition with my paycheck and also because for him it was easy money.

We got off about the same time because of him, he wanted this, and after work which was about 9 pm I would prepare his dinner and run a bath for him and or get his things prepared for a shower I washed and folded his clothes.

Our mornings would be like this; I would wake up hours before him so to prepare for **his** day.

My narc liked his coffee every morning, before anything. He spoke of his dad being this most wonderful guy; however, I pictured just the opposite according to his examples.

I believe the mother of a NARC has to be a very miserable person with a very selfish spouse. In essence picturing the dad being the king narcissist who has raised more than one Narc.

I believe when a Narc says they look up to a parent, in my opinion that parent, the one the Narc speaks of, is the reason for his pain and that parent is the King Narc and is the reason for child's inability to change.

As I stated my Narc loved his coffee in the morning as I did, the difference with him is that he would want his coffee freshly ground every day, I wouldn't even think so much about that only he would have me get his creamer from one store and his coffee from another, because he would say," all creamers do not taste the same".

My narc never thought of my day or if I was tired or even if there was something he could do for me.

Sometimes I would make his coffee with regular coffee and creamer he never even knew the difference.

After researching I later to found out he would go up north for coffee because there was a married woman he would visit and buy gifts for that he was grooming and having sex with. **(While married)** This woman later divorced her husband, this is sad in itself.

When I began to get suspicious of his personality and behaviors is when he would leave an hour or two before work claiming to be working out, but he was not at the gym.

Weekly, I would cut the grass we had huge piece of land with mature trees and precise landscaping.

When I cut the grass he would sometimes fuss, but he would never want to cut the grass, so if I did not do the yard would look horrible.

Before the mask came off, almost every evening he would drink wine sometimes liquor.

One evening he pulled out his gun he had purchased to protect the house, and began pointing at himself, it had no bullets in it, and it freaked me out I yelled and told him to stop he then pointed it at me, and because I trusted him, I felt like he would never hurt me, so I blew him off and told him to stop, he did and put the gun up. I thought nothing of it because he was drinking.

The second time this happened, I became very nervous because he was a little bit tipsy, but I still blew it off to the drinking, not his actual self. In retrospect I now believe he was practicing maybe hurting me, Hinds sight is 20/20.

One of our mutual friends approached me and said he was a smoker, my response was he does not smoke, she then said, yes he does, so I walked over to him with her and asked him if he smokes and he lied and said he just started smoking again. In fact, he had never stopped smoking he would just hide it from me.

This was when things changed, Someone came to me and said he was cheating and I just could not believe it because he was so good to me, I just did not care to hear it in fact I just ignored the comment. While not wanting to believe what this good friend had mentioned to me I began to watch his behaviors. While observing him, I noticed that he did not want to go out anymore like to dinner his excuse was he works too much and that he was tired. If I were to put up a fuss about spending the time, he would get so mad that his rage did not match the actual situation.

These behaviors began to make me pay attention even more. During this time he had secretly removed me from his credit cards and also removed my access from our cell phone account, so I had no access to get records, so he thought. Not know he had made these secret moves of removing me from the account my intuition was steering my thoughts, so I watched his spending habits and his personality, I noticed that he wanted to have flashy things this was so strange because he told me he does not like flashy things. I ask him to buy a car because he was making me drive his old car while he drove my newer car and I worked hard I knew we had the money, so I asked him he immediately said no. So I went and bought me a car because I did not feel his reasoning was correct. I still included him, and he literally embarrassed me so bad at the car lot and insisted he go on the loan.

I am sharing these details to show you the behaviors and to show you how easy it is to dismiss it and feel guilty for making decisions to better your life while with these individuals.

(The scenarios suggest narcissistic behaviors in its truest form.)

Still watching his behavior I noticed he had blocked me from Social media, I thought to myself who blocks their wife from Facebook, at this point I am convinced but afraid to look at his computer for fear of what I might find. As I am driving down the street, I notice a notification on my phone from our phone service which said that my narc had removed me from the shared phone account as an administrator, which we shared this responsibility from day one. When asking him why he removed me he responded that I had done something that I should not have done. Honestly I cannot even remember what it was, he also stated, that I was not responsible, so he wants to take control of it. The real reason was he felt me realizing who he really was so he removed me from the account so that I would know about the co-worker he was calling at 4 am and the other women he was seeing outside of the marriage.

(The Day of no more guessing)

I decided not to go to work one day, and I looked on his computer there were pictures (we all know what that means) of multiple women there were intimate conversations there were pictures of women in his clothes there was evidence that at least one of them had sex in our house we shared together there were comments like him saying he loved them just like he told me, he would even date them, and take to the same place he proposed to me. Realizing I was not safe at all, in fact, I was living with the enemy.

The masked was removed, after I looked at this mess, I printed everything and pulled all phone records. I let him know what I knew and his first words were "what have you done" not I am sorry or how can I fix this or even tears just "what have you done" then he began to continue to carry on with these women and telling them how I am mean to him and how I am a horrible wife the same story he was feeding me about his ex and how she cheated on him.(again this is not my life just a story told) However, the day before I removed his mask, I was the love of his life.

    Understanding He told people things about me way before things hit the fan to make his story seem believable, so many horrible things here is the most important piece to all of this he showed NO remorse, and he took NO ownership. I tried to offer to counsel and also tried to figure what was going on, he just kept toying with my emotions sayings like he would do counseling and that being stressed with the bills, made him say, "Fuck it". However the day before I found his truth, I was "The Love of his Life" and he was "the happiest he had ever been in his life" I was confused, feeling so abandoned even though I was leaving, and although he left me way before I physically left our home. Feeling abandoned emotionally and left with so many unanswered questions such as:

Why did he even pursue me?

Why would he marry me?

How could he hurt me?

Whenever I would try to get answers, he would be so rude, as if he never cared for me at all, creating a sense of self-doubt for me, and also the false sense that he was the victim, and one would think I had cheated on him.

Once he told me... "he and my ex-were friends and that God himself could not bring him back to me."

He also had one of his girlfriend's better, yet sources call me before we were even divorced now I knew this was no one he intended on keeping this was someone to heal the wound and feed his ego through this time because he knew he was done with me because I knew his truth.

(I want you to pay attention to the signs and how a person can make excuse for a person's horrible behaviors)

He knew I would never view him the same way. I was devastated; I could not believe I had fell in love with such a vile person. After finding this out and realizing there is no hope, immediately I filed for termination of the commitment and moved out of the home. I made many mistakes during this phase like trying to work it out or even considering counseling he said yes and he knew would never go to counseling. He was as rude as a person could be to his significant other speaking with no feeling and sometimes he would come home from work and go outside to smoke a cigarette and be on "what's app" talking to one of the females. She would send me their messages telling her he felt threatened for his life. I could not believe it, I was devastated, and I felt like I could just die. How could he have fooled me like this?

How could someone do this to a woman?

Well, this how he could do this to me because I was nothing, to begin with, and he never looked at me as anything other an object, and he discarded me way before I ever left.

He tried on many occasions before I left to make me feel like, it was my fault too and to make me feel guilty.

I would get so angry with this individual that breaking tables or yelling became an everyday thing for several months. Panic- attacks were happening daily for me. Here is where the problem sits when you have been abused the abusers knows what he or she has done, they know what state you are going to be at each stage of the whole ordeal, so they know you will feel abandoned they also know you will want them back. In knowing you will try to come back, so they wait for it so that they can hurt you more.

This also happened to me, I felt like this has to be a mistake I know he loves me if I could have a conversation with him he will at least realize, I told myself, I will be the bigger person and just apologize for whatever I had done to make him unhappy, and I am willing to work this out. I asked him was it, my kids, he absolutely not. I do not think I have ever felt this low in my life. This by far was the worst thing had happened to in my life.

(Author insight)

I am only sharing this story with you because maybe you can see yourself in this story and if you do,

Knowing you are not alone is so important.

I want you to stop blaming yourself or to question your ability to be a good wife is not an option. If you see yourself in this story you were not the problem, you have been used and indeed toyed with, and there was no way of knowing because these types of individuals do not attack your intelligence, they attack your heart.

This book is to allow you to see/know who they are alert your senses to their foolishness so you can move forward and on to the success God has for you. My

<u>goal is to **EMPOWER** you through my words.</u>

(The fight back begins)

Being hurt to the core, never given any closure, this is when I had enough, no more starting over, no more losing from this day forward I am going to fight, and I am going to win. This type of pain will make you decide to win.

Fight with success! You have to first look at all your flaws and mistakes that you have made up until this point. Pay attention to why you are making these mistakes. You have to reveal your authentic self, to yourself.

Revealing my most vulnerable secrets to you, secrets of what made me have low self-esteem to the point that I felt like I would give another person control over my life as if they know better than me, what is right for me. This is a pathetic mindset, and it is lazy it is also unattractive. When you display such weak tendencies, Narcissists can spot you a mile away.

My Authentic Self!

I come from an abusive family; I was raised by an abusive father and a passive mother. My dad uses to beat my mother until she was unrecognizable, my dad tried to kill my mother and siblings when we were all under ten years old.

I was almost rape at 8-years old by a stranger just a few doors from my house, and a neighbor saved me. I struggled with this all through my life years with learning disabilities and work as it was hard for me to focus.

Until this point of my life, as it pertains to relationships, my reality was that the one person that is supposed to make you feel safe has abused my mother and threat the whole family.

I was somewhat confused, afraid of my own father, he was the only example of relationships I had seen until I was in my teens.

Making the mistake of getting pregnant the same year I was to graduate, made my graduation challenging and also made my ability to walk across the stage impossible according to the high school. Because of this, I was mad at myself for 10 years until finally, I decided to get my life, by this time I had gotten married to someone that was abusive; however abuse was familiar, common, almost expected so having three children by the time I was 21, life was off to a rocky start.

    My first marriage we were both young and had gone through some things as children so I do not blame him now but then, I just tried to fight back. When I reflect I could have made better decisions hinds sight is 20/20. This abusive marriage lasted for 16years, part of the abuse was verbal, physical, mostly things like "you will ever be nothing" "No one's going to want you with three kids" He would leave and be gone for days come back and say he was at his brother's house. Finding ways to focus because I had a verbally abusive and physically abusive person in my life at the time of taking the test and now my children had the same experience as me. During my college years, I also got a real estate license and began to learn the business. My major was International Business, having a particular interest in the French language.

(The vision here even though you are in the midst of a storm continue to build a career even if you not sure when and how you will use it)

Growing up, the clarity of having direction or even a sense of creating goals for my life never even existed. Hell, feeling safe was never known to me as a child or an adult. My first husband cheated my second husband cheated.

Taking full responsibility for my actions, choices, and my mistakes, please don't misunderstand my openness; the purpose of this exercise is to show you what revealing all of your flaws and to being as open to you as I was to what sounds like my significant other at the time so you can see how this makes one vulnerable to this type of induvial such as a narcissist.

(I need you to feel the vulnerability in my actions.)

Having no vision at all from the moment I became an adult and no sense of what to do or where I was going no plan at all. Low self-esteem and abuse were my foundation. Not knowing who I was or where I was going, this is a narcissistic playground. Feeling pretty was never a part of my young life; however, I was shapely and attractive to most and in shape most of my life.

After buying a home and getting my real estate license, I finally began to have a glimpse of my worth. Still not realizing or having clarity of how valuable I am, I was beginning, to believe I have the ability to be whatever I want to be. To say I didn't have ambition as a young child would be false; however ambition is nothing if you do not believe in yourself, or if you have a low self-concept.

At this point in my life low self-concept and low self- esteem, was the case but I had lots of ambition, with no believe in myself.

Driving a nice car and buying home. In saying that you should know, having a nice car and buying a home is a great thing but I had no real focus, direction, or sense of maintaining proper credit, I was living from pay to paycheck because of my poor decisions.

Having not been taught how to maintain proper credit or the importance of this because the most important thing my mother focused on was putting food on the table and keeping the lights on.

On a scholarship and to get away from my life, I went to college in Paris France for a little while at "the Sorbonne" where I did pretty well actually because I was away from the noise. I still could not hear God.

Being stuck in pain, **(I need you to hear what I just said really.)**

"I was stuck in pain" Having a continuous lonely heart, and not accomplishing my goals, my mind was stuck in a mess, continuously trying to figure a way, of how to get out.

Do not ever get stuck this satanic play;

It is a way to keep you from becoming what God has for you to become.

While reading this, try to connect with the feelings and the place I found myself in the unfortunate decisions and excuse I came up with because of my poor decisions, use this as a way to recognize your feelings. This will help you become a stronger person so you can recognize and protect yourself and your dreams from not only temptations of life and our poor decision making but also narcissistic characteristics and notice when someone has poor intentions of your life.

This is the part of my life that made me who I am today. My voice is the truth unapologetic and fearless of your judgment. I want to help you; I want to help you see that you can make mistakes but learn faster than I did let me help you through my truth

and wisdom move you forward with confidence and grace.

So my second Significant other brought me to my knees, which I am confident makes him so happy because that was the goal he wanted to destroy me.

My second Commitment forced me to fight from a new place; the pain was so thick that it felt like it took a part of my soul, nothing has ever hurt me like this or made me feel so disrespected, betrayed, defeated or deceived; my commitment meant the world to me. The Termination of the commitment meant even more. Telling the truth and being authentic frees my soul.

I enjoy being transparent without malice. What does it mean to bet being authentic has done for me is so compelling I have to share this feeling this energy that makes you free. Now success!

2017 was the birth of my brokerage, 2017 was the birth my consulting service.

I want you to embrace your mistakes embrace your fears embrace who you are and love every bit of it.

I am a divorced newlywed who had no clue what I was dealing with, and I take full responsibility for moving too fast, for wanting to believe instead of doing my homework.

I accept the fact that I could have made a better decision and it is ok.

Revealing my authentic self, helped me forgive, it was my awakening. I hope it helps you connect with your ability fight and know how setbacks and pain play a significant role in your destiny, of which I like to call your success.

My mistakes have given me a clear direction, with clear goals, combined with a fierce determination to get to the finish line.

My primary focus is to help someone have the same clarity, and to fight for what is already yours.

Live authentically with boundaries, loving yourself entirely means to love your mistakes and your accomplishments.

Love yourself not for anyone but you, and do this on purpose.

Now that you have written down all your flaws, now we can begin.

Understanding the pain Now you can grow!

Chapter 3

The Awakening of your authentic self, forgiving, and moving on

<u>Do you know what it means to be authentic?</u>

To be authentic means that you expose the truth about yourself to whomever you are speaking to. So for example, in this book, I told the world my truth. I allowed the world inside of my innermost secrets things that I would hide for fear that you might not like me or even ridicule. I told you the good and bad about me, held back nothing.

When you are authentic you are expressing your core self, morals and values excellent and sorry it is just you and who you are what you like, what you do not like. Authentic self is who you are. Like it or not this is who I am unapologetically. Be yourself. This is your truth and it and will set you free.

When you are authentic, it can feel so liberating, because there are no lies, or fear, being authentic is a way of saying you love yourself.

Accepting your flaws and mistakes can be challenging.

I had a hard time with this because I made so many bad choices that led me to many setbacks, but each one of those setbacks has prepared me for this very moment.

(GIVING YOU SOME TOOLS)

So let's begin, I want to teach you tools to help you with being authentic. Self-esteem should be supported so if you have some emotional baggage give it the time that it needs then get rid of it and move on. Self-doubt is no longer a part of your life at this point; from this day forward you are expressing who you are at the core in detail with no shame for the purpose of self-development and self-acceptance. It is challenging to act right to your personality when you have self-doubt, or when you lie to yourself and to others. So I need you to be honest at this moment and from now on really. Let go of all the hurt and pain, at the same time; I want you to embrace it and don't be ashamed of it. I want you to begin to entertain the thought of believing in yourself, loving yourself. You know how you feel when you are around your parents that the feeling of self, that you do not have to be ON for anyone you can just relax. These are the feelings I need you to connect with. While you are connecting with these feelings, I want you to think about how kind you are, and how loving your spirit is, also, how good you are as a person. I want you to think about how compassionate you are, remember your dreams as you visualized them from a child. When you are alone how at peace are you? Think about how great it is to be you. Support your self-esteem daily.

As you are connecting with these emotions, pay specific attention to your vision write your vision down on paper.

Next, I want you to think about your beliefs; authentic people have their own beliefs; and morals without the influence of their parents or friends. Once you have explored your beliefs and morals. I want you to write them down; this is where and how boundaries are established in my opinion. So with your beliefs; and good morals saying no should be easy for you when it's aginst what you stand for.

Good morals and beliefs make you who you are they keep you grounded, stay true to yourself always. Church and school also our parents are examples of things that influence us to form ethical standards and morals. These influences are distorted they can have an adverse effect as well.

Personal Development is next, Take a class or start a business; you know what you like so just take action on yourself. This is where you begin to focus on you and to add value to yourself. Adding value to yourself is a great way to find out what makes you happy as you develop your skills and honestly get to know yourself. Even as I write this book I and adding value to myself and also getting to know myself at the same time. This is a never-ending process you will never fully know yourself in my opinion.

Evaluate your job and make sure you love what you do If when you assess your job, you find that you are not happy to take action and fix this immediately. This can be challenging for someone who does not believe in themselves or if you are not sure of what really makes you happy. If you find yourself having these feelings I want you to make no decision about this until you are sure and or fearless. If your decision is to quit then make sure you educate yourself on the next move or even educate yourself on the consequences, so you are prepared. Always leave on good terms, and this will also discard of any anxiety you may be having which help you have clear more focused thoughts.

Do not quit your current job until you have found the job you will love doing. Most people quit their jobs and then find a job exactly like the one they just left lol, please don't do this. I have explored many jobs; I always come back to the same thing, which is what I love to do for that is real estate and motivating people, inspiring people has always been my dream job.

As a child, I could visualize myself running my own company I could see the house my house was going to look. I could see it so clearly. Imagining my success was like having cable tv, or riding your favorite bike, for me as a child. Even today the visuals to happen, I can see my life through vision.

Honesty is; next, this is also important, you must be an honest person to like yourself. Liking yourself is the key to your self-esteem and to your overall character as it relates to relationships, your self-thoughts and ultimately to your success.

When you describe yourself do not use harmful words always say good positive things about yourself this is very important to your future because you are what you think about. What you think so shall you be.

All of the theories being discussed, you have heard before however now you can listen to what is being said because you have gone through some things and life has called your attention.

Accept your flaws, and do not be a fake person. Identify with any triggers that allowed you to get into specific situations that led you to this point of loss of self.

If you are overweight, accept it if you do not like it change it. If you failed a test admit it, don't lie about it study and pass the next one. Trust yourself, know that you are human and you will make mistakes also when you make a decision on something trust your self-being in this state of being its ok to believe in yourself be you are aware of your actions and know that you are not making stupid moves.

Trust yourself that whatever you press upon to do trust that you can do it. Being authentic means if you need help you are not ashamed to ask for it. Forgiving is challenging but necessary take your time with this because it has to be real the forgiveness. To be authentic don't say you have forgiven someone until you **really have.**

When you have forgiven them you will know it takes time. In the meantime, focus on yourself, focus on your dreams and your goals, and stay as busy as you possibly can with a clear path and clear plan. The way to start this process is to find time to get away from everything.

During this discovery time you have to have no noise, for a more than a few moments to try to get away from everyone to get your thoughts transparent so that you can look at your life and your passion without any noise or distractions. At this point, you will begin to understand the clarity of your life, and you can start to develop a plan to get back to you and your goals.

When you get this moment of clarity, you may shed a few tears because this moment is your awakening moment. This moment is the moment of pure authenticity because God begins to work on your soul and you are basically at his mercy you have tried everything on your own, and you have failed. Now it is time to surrender to his will so he can heal your heart and give you the life that is designed for you. This is the moment of pure authenticity.

Moving on after this becomes easier because you know it is over at this point and you know, who you are, at this point; you now realize you have the biggest fight of your life. The difference in this fight versus all others is that you are determined to win so you are strategizing, planning, you are goal driven, this time you are focused.

There are no more chances to give. You are now aware of the games; you are focused like never before. This was God's plan; he knew it could not happen any other way. You are destined for greatness!

Moving on is nothing short of a fight, it takes skill and is forever. Moving on requires you eliminate all memories of the negative forces, it requires you to become numb to the mess.

So too indeed move on you must clean the slate so to speak, you are being reborn, no more speaking of the negative force no more procrastination.

At this point in your life even if you are 75 years old, it does not matter this is the fight of your life. I need you to fight for your soul right now and forever. This fight means everything. There is no room for losing because you have something to prove right now and forever in this fight! That is what moving on means today and forever.

When **God** has blessed you enough to get out of all the mess you have put yourself in, you better fight for the second chance he so graciously gave you, and by God, you will win!

Pace yourself think about every move you make. When making important decisions that will affect your life long term, use slow thinking and really look at every aspect of the choices you make to assure a good outcome. Be present, this means to be in the moment really this will help you to appreciate the fact you are still here in the land of the living, this will also help you to value your time.

Be present when you have a birthday parties for your mother or your grandchildren these are special moments, this is moving on.

Appreciate the moments you share with your family.

The family is your foundation it keeps you grounded. When we lose focus of our foundation, we lose ourselves, and we also lose authenticity. The family is a part of your authenticity. Being authentic is a necessity to finding yourself especially when you have experienced abuse or even when you have just utterly lost your way.

Moving on requires prayer, and determination, you will need to pray for your soul, and you are the strength to continue the journey with courage and a never quit mentality. Pray for the people that have hurt you and thank God for your second chance. Thank God for the healthy sharp mind you have and also your health in general. This is how you begin every day. **Remember to pray and ask God to help you** never forget to thank him for his mercy and grace that he has bestowed upon you, God is going to bless you, and is praising you right now just by reading this book. This book is the bridge to your success, so thank him at this moment.

Chapter 4

Focusing on you, rebuilding your future, and getting rid of the pain.

Thinking about the things you always wanted to do when you were a child is the same as going back to your roots so to speak. Think about all your good qualities and think about how other people see you.

When you think about your life and your setbacks, what is the constant in your life? For me for example, when I think about my life I ever since and even before my 20's, I have always wanted to be a leader in public speaking or running a company. My thoughts were If I were not getting paid, I would love to run my own successful company with a substantial gorgeous office with people working there and helping others and providing for their families leaving a legacy of greatness. Now honestly the thought was not so wordy, but when explaining how much I enjoy encouraging people to be authentic, there are not enough words to describe that for me. Public speaking, I love it hell just speaking with meaning or purpose I love. Speaking with purpose is so powerful, helping people to grow and find their happiness and success this is my dream true.

Although money is necessary, this should not be the primary focus.

I want you to begin to focusing on increasing your income passively, but with direction. While reading this book hopefully you are taking notes, but if you have not, I want you to take notes from this point on. Today and every day from this point on I want you to become more productive and present in everything you do.

Today I want you to write down all the goals you want to accomplish this year. I want you to write down how you are going to do this. How are you going to make money to accomplish the goals? I also want you to write down the date that you are going to accomplish the goals. (In this book I have provided space for you to write this down.) To continue, write down what problem you can solve to make this money? Write down what does financial freedom mean to you and what does passive income mean to you. For me, a passive stream of income is writing this book. I look at passive income as income that comes with little or no effort, with a continuous flow of income, after the work is complete.

To have this kind of thought process make no mistake, you are beginning to feel stronger and in control of your life. This process is giving you clarity through prayer, and knowledge, and self-awareness.

Once you have moved on leaving any abuse or bad behaviors behind you will begin to, in fact, other people are beginning to see and notice your strength and you are talking and walking with confidence. Can you see it? Planning your future requires vision you have to see your future as you want it to be before you can actually move towards it then you have to create a plan as to how you are going to reach your goals.

What are these things that are blocking you from accomplishing your goals? Financial freedom is when your income surpasses your debt x 10. Knowing this, how can you get your income to surpass you debt x 10? Now you are starting from a place of a target instead of starting without a target.

"The beginning of Creating wealth"

Let's begin to map this out. Multiple streams of income are required to do this now what does this look like. For me it looks like I will write books selling e-books, I have an online business, I will have more than one business, and I am working a full-time job to start. E-books and online businesses are called passive income.

Passive income is income received with little effort on a regular basis; little effort does not mean easy. You have to create several streams of income with a set target for the week the month and the year.

Now to begin you may not reach any of your targets, but over time you will begin to hit your targets, so I want you to aim for the target. Financial freedom is an illusion financial skill and confidence is real. This is what you are aiming for "Financial confidence." –Dan Lok.

I believe in order to have order one has to evaluate everything that has happened good and bad in their lives. Evaluating the relationships is a critical part of your life. You must

Understanding-

reflect on how you were feeling about yourself when the relationships began.

Look at the mistakes you made while in the relationships this is a crucial factor in your self-esteem and making sure you have no more setbacks.

Your life and death depend on your future decisions, so there is no room for mistakes at this point.

Use the wisdom of your past to make sure you are fully healed and have a sharp mind. Unshakeable and prayed up, before you begin making long-term decisions for your life.

When you are entertaining the thought of dating a person, use your wisdom to see who the person is past the surface really. This prepares you for your new business ventures you are about to have. Take your time with relationships pay attention to how fast they are trying to move, ultimately pay attention to how fast they say they love you, pay attention to how fast they want to entertain the idea of sex. This speaks volumes do not ignore your instincts. What you will produce next in your life will depend on whether or not you practice self-discipline and good self-evaluation.

Take time to heal from all the pain and hurt, getting rid of the pain takes a few simple steps.

Some people need this and some people don't but it a necessary process to get rid of the old baggage before and in order to take new on successes.

At this moment I want you to think about the first step which is forgiveness.

When you forgive you free yourself from the hold the other person has on you.

Pursue God

Now, I know people say this all the time, what I want you to do at this moment is just take a few deep breaths, and take your time, be present in this moment, really think about what a needed person you are, also think about God and peace.

I believe God is present right now at this moment using these words for me to let you know he loves you and you are here for a reason.

I believe surrendering to the mercy of God. Having humility and faith that God is about to take you to the next level and chapter of your life and the people who hurt you and set you back are not allow in this moment you can take a few moments before you read further and shed a tear say a prayer, I just want you to feel this moment and experience it to the fullest indeed.

Forgive yourself for not being where you wanted to be at this point in your life and know your time is now. I want you to forgive yourself allowing people in that didn't deserve in your space, thank God for teaching you that lesson and take the tools he has given you and protect your heart. I want you to know its ok have faith. Letting will free your soul so you can heal.

Going through these moments more than once or twice will make you a stronger more focused machine you will feel stronger, and you will know you are ready to make decisions and handle your blessings.

What is it to be fully fledged? To be full-fledged means to be fully developed, full grown. In this thing called life, sometimes we got hurt and broken into small pieces. Life can pluck at you until you have nothing left. If you fight through and come out on the other side, I am proof that God will be waiting for you on the other side. If you think you can make it in this life without God, you need to think again. You need to think and have you be in his word in order to make it.

New beginnings/ New Ventures New Possibilities

Entrepreneurship is what I believe God had for me, even as a child I knew this would be part of my growth. Small medium enterprise entrepreneurship (SME) focuses on local market; this is my real estate firm **Rhynehardt & Associates LLC,** Innovation-Driven

Enterprise Entrepreneurship, (IDE) is where my consulting firm Bossed Up Entrepreneur Consulting LLC falls into because this is a much broader business reaching people all over the world. Helping people is the most rewarding thing you can do for yourself. Helping people is better than money. Earlier I mentioned that I am a focused machine, it comes from helping people. Helping people is therapeutic. You want to focus on yourself and become more one with everything, center yourself, I use to hear people say that and I would laugh now I get it. I have seen people who are not at peace with themselves; they think they are too fat they think they are not happy with themselves or where they are in life. I was that person; all that needs to be said about this is, just know this is noise. It's the kind of noise that will kill your dream.

You are nothing short of perfection. Getting rid of the pain in your heart if any to move on is understanding what you were dealing with, and know if you lose they win. That can't happen to me. So at this moment evaluate yourself once again and look deep into the mistakes you made and realize that it's ok.

Eliminate the negative people, the negative vibes and always follow your instincts. Instincts tell you when you have bad friends and instincts warn you of dangerous people it's like a dogs 6th sense it's a gift from God listen to it always.

Chapter 5

Self-training, clarity, and understanding and why you were chosen.

It's time to be happy you have made all the mistakes after being discarded by a narcissist the mistakes are over. Understanding who you are is nothing short of being clear about whom you are and why you are why you can't hold that job and why you do not happen. In knowing who you are, if you are not doing what you were put on this earth to do your heart will never be satisfied, you will work, but you will never give 100%. It is time to find your purpose, the way to do that is to understand your core value. What is the one thing you love and support and or your dream life or job? These things are essential to understanding what your purpose is and understanding your purpose helps you to forgive others and become free of your pain. Look at what you have enjoyed from a child; can you make this a business? For me, it's helping people find themselves. I have loved this since I was a child. I remember I had a neighbor she was even less fortunate than me which was pretty bad I could tell her self-esteem was low, and her self-worth was invisible. So I began to give her my clothes and do her hair and even allow her to take a bath at my house so she could merely feel pretty or feel good about herself. This gift to her was so rewarding to me I knew I wanted to do this for someone else. This feeling is who I am, my authentic self, without any influence or interruption.

When I was a child, eight years old, a paper route was my life. My mother instilled work and hustle at a young age. This is where the business side comes into play for me. My mother would get us up at 4 am, and my siblings and I would be out delivering papers and expanding our route with marketing. The purpose of this route was to make money to buy the things that mother couldn't take the burden off of her. It was the best thing ever. Delivering papers was liberating.

There is nothing you can't accomplish in this life with the right amount of work. You have to get rid of the fear of failure because it merely keeps you stuck. Don't be lazy please don't be lazy there is someone that needs your talent. I have been used, disrespected, cheated on, laughed at, and abandoned I have had nothing short of a hard time but never has quitting been an option. I refuse to fail and prove my haters right. One of my closest relatives hates my hustle or me so much they would rather trust another person to sell their home than to trust their own blood who has their best interest at heart.

Believe this it's nothing short of hate and this hurts because they want you to feel like you are not good enough. Pray for your haters like that, family or not this should make you hustler harder because your family is jealous of your progress not only are they jealous but they are intimidated by your growth. Your haters will even tell others not to use you and why they won't use your services which in my opinion are very sad because it can hurt your business, which are their intentions. Never let people or their thoughts about you affect your hustle pray for them. These people are usually miserable, self-centered people who look good on the exterior but on the inside are sad, pitiful individuals. Everything you do when it comes to your purpose will be challenging, make no mistake.

Self-training for me begins with self-confidence. Fear holds us back more than anything else. I came from a poor family, and I know my mother had low esteem, so this began with my mother. Low self-esteem and low self-confidence really can determine the direction of your life so you must get control of this out the gate. Confidence affects how we live our lives how we marry, how we do business, everything that is necessary for business depends on confidence. Confidence is appealing to others self-confidence is vital.

As individuals doubt, fear is the most significant problem we have as people; guilt and unworthiness and the feelings of inferiority and self-worthiness are also problems as it pertains to how we live our lives. Think about the things you would have accomplished in life if you take away fear. Thoughts are causes and conditions are effects. When you have low self-esteem, you are opening yourself to people to take advantage of you, so it is imperative that you get control of your esteem and how you feel about yourself. The law of belief is whatever you believe with feeling becomes your reality. The code of opinion is compelling. Don't allow people like a narcissist to come into your life and break your will and or change your belief of yourself through their treatment of you without self-confidence and self-esteem you will be a target. What is your view of yourself? Make it suitable for example my self-believe that I can do whatever I want and I am a success. I believe I am destined for success and everything I go through is my preparation for my success. I am worthy.

You must have excellent powerful thoughts about yourself and your life. When you are a person of substance, people have to treat you as such. You have to know, that you know, that you are deserving of being treated like the high-quality person you are.

For example, when you purchase a home versus an apartment, you have to maintain that house you have to give it the proper attention so that it holds its value. When you are leasing an apartment, you do not care about this place because you probably won't keep it; This is the exact description of what individuals suffering with a narcissistic personality disorder. You have to love yourself enough to know your value and your worth.

When you know your worth, you are not attractive to nonsense. This book is to help you realize who you are through insight and wisdom. After reading this book even if you feel strong and on top of your game you must take a vacation alone not too far away, but somewhere you feel safe, and you let it be you and God.

I use this exercise in every book because my goal is to get you to focus on your purpose and I cannot get you to do this if your mind is cloudy or if there is noise. I need you to be in a place where you cannot run an errand or pick up the kids nothing just silences. Now what I am going to tell you to do next is going to sound crazy, but it will be refreshing and liberating.

Pursue God:

I want you to talk to God about all your mistakes. Next, I want you to write down your errors then I want you to cry and let it all out just let it go, now I want you to tear this list up and flush it down the toilet, now I want you to make another list of all your accomplishments and everything you have been through good and complicated that you have overcome, this list will make you smile and it might even make you cry as well, but this time the tears will be of joy. In this list, you will realize just who you are.

I do not even know you, but I bet this list is pretty amazing. Now you know your worth. Soon you can begin to see yourself how others see you. More importantly, it will help you to understand others differently as well.

These mental exercises such as controlling how you think for example: If you believe that your life is going to turn out well, it will. Always expect the best of yourself and your life and everything you do. Call success to yourself.

Positive thoughts are essential to your success. Parents hope your kids to do well and they will rise to your expectations. These are tools to help you keep a positive self-concept. If you are married tell your spouse you believe in them this is the best thing you can do for them and your marriage what happens is, you inspire the need to prove you right, to make you proud. These exercises help you and your relationships with others.

Self-evaluation is a must before you get on to the person God is creating in you. He has you reading this book to make sure that whatever he has planned for your life will never be stolen from you. So yes he allowed you to go through some things, so you know what that feels and also so you know you without a doubt it is not for you.

God is making you unshakeable. So what are we talking about let's regroup this talk is about self-confidence and how you feel about yourself, how people try to break you how this affects your growth. Fear and low self-worth can stop your blessing. When you get these thoughts I want you redirected your thoughts and speak to yourself loving, and powerful thinking like this,

"I love my life, I am leaving a great legacy for my family. I am proud of my accomplishments, and I am proud of my mistakes, I know God loves me and success is walking with me. God has something great for my life; he is helping people through me. I am

thankful to God for my life and my work"

Repeat these thoughts over and over again until the negative thinking is gone and get back to the business at hand. Your self-concept always has to be great. Your self-concept/self-image is how you think about yourself. Controlling the negative thought is a must.

Controlling your thoughts comes with clarity of your life. Having and setting goals, give clarity to your life. Goals determine the trajectory of your life. The words "I like myself" improve the way you feel about yourself, just like "goal setting " gives structure and direction. Controlling your thoughts is vital concerning the negative forces in your life. You are To do and become something great, God chose you to read this book, you didn't just by chance pick this book to read, no he wanted you, to help you move forward, with all the distractions that come in our lives you have to engage with the mental food that you need to stay focused and to stay inspired to be great. Make time to feed your mind and spirit; it is your duty to live a good life.

In this section of the book I want you to focus on your Goals, write down 10 things you want to accomplish this year.

1._____
2._____
3._____
4._____
5._____
6._____
7._____
8._____
9._____
10._____

Now I want you to write down how you are going to accomplish these goals. With completion date

1._____

2._____

3._____

4._____

5._____

6._____

7._____

8._____

9._____

10._____

In my opinion, growth is in knowledge but you have to be open to things that use to different and uncommon.

Doing things different may often include God and his guidance, protection and prayer. I need you to connect with that feeling because knowing that you cannot do anything without God is a good place to be mentally.

Chapter 6

Success & living your life pain-free, with no more setbacks.

Success is not about money, even though money helps, success is about happiness, the kind of happiness that makes you proud to be you. When you marry someone it makes you feel happy, but not like the kind of happiness you get when you pass a test or get a promotion.

The kind of happiness that comes from a promotion is self-inflicted, it's earned, and it makes you feel proud, it empowers you, and improves your self-esteem improves your self-concept.

Knowing this helps not only someone but helps you to understand who you are and what makes you happy. Knowing this allows one to know you can't rely on someone else to make you happy, knowing this helps to prevent you from becoming a victim. Only you can make you happy. This took me a long, long time to learn and cost me many mistakes. Living pain-free for some may mean they don't have any aches in their body lol, but the pain I am discussing is the pain of not being satisfied with who you are.

 The pain I am discussing is the pain from a broken heart. Living pain-free means you are completely satisfied with who you are and you are thriving, not surviving. When a person is thriving, it looks like this: one might be working hard every day, cleaning up their credit if they need to, buying a house, writing a book, starting a business, traveling, and just simply enjoying life with a peace of mind. Peacefully, and indirectly, fighting back against everything and everyone who tried to destroy them is thriving. Never quitting on yourself never even saying the word quit empowers you even more! Living your life, for yourself is thriving.

So how do you prevent yourself from having setbacks? Setbacks of low self-esteem after a failed relationship or being let go from a job someone passing away etc. loss comes in many forms there is no preparation for death in my opinion. How does one maintain the happiness and the progress they have made in life?

Protect /Rediscover

Preventing setbacks is in the **expecting** of setbacks goal setting and the deadlines for the goals, creating multiple streams of good income, these things ensure control of your life. Do not set up streams of income that is not profitable, create streams of income that bring you good money, don't waste your time. Rediscover yourself.

Rediscovering yourself requires one to explore your **truth**. Who you really are takes lots of failing. Failing makes you dig deep, failing takes you to a place that is supernatural. At some point you will fail so hard that it will be enough to take you higher when you are there NOTHING will stop you. As you become who you were meant to be you will find that you want to do bigger and bolder that desire to win over takes your soul.

I like to call it God taking you to your destiny. You will realize this was all

God's plan he knew because of your truth and who you really are without this type of failing you would not believe in yourself, you would not have the faith in him, and also you would still be living and reliving that awful cycle of abuse which is a downward cycle to destruction.

I hope this book helps you to connect with progression moving forward. If that happens while reading this book even in the slightest bit, I have done my job. Thank you for reading the book God blessed. Again reading this book more than once is the way to gaining the most from experience.

Food for Thought:

>Ways to become a Millionaire!

Do The Math:

1. One Million dollars divided by 450 is $2,222.. What can you sell for $2,222 450 times which would make you a millionaire!

2. One Million dollars Divided by 650 is $1538.46 what service could you provided 650 times at $1538.46 in 12 months that would make you a Millionaire!

BOSS UP!

Poem

I'm not there yet! –

Popular & sexy is what he could see,

Classy, & Assy yeah that's me,

He came out the blue so sexy, yeah it felt true,

Said all the right words, did all the right things,

This can't be real.... it has to be a dream

Met my mother and my father,

Yeah, he checked out well,

Except for my father,

he said to go to hell,

No signs of deceit, no signs he would cheat,

He held me so tight, and he held me all night,

I will never, forget because it felt so right,

His skin so flawless, beautiful, and dark,

After some thought Man this guy is a NARC.

He was so good, so smooth and so quick,

He had nothing to say when

I caught him in his shit,

Just lie after lie a covert from the start,

How was I to know, this Joker was a Narc!

Why is it so hard for a man to treat a woman right?

Just to be faithful, and come home at night,

Can't you see what it does to a woman's soul?

Oh, that's right you're a Narc until you're old.

Your family has always known exactly who you are

When you married me, they thought

Not again

OH MY GOD!

Living your life inflicting so much pain,

Hopefully, your daughter won't have to experience the same thing.

Made a joke of my life yeah even made bets,

My fight back is not complete,

I'm just saying ……."I'm not there yet!"

This girl, that woman,

Yeah, you all laughed and giggled

When the mask came off

They all said the same thing,

"You can have him he's SOO little."

At the gym writing books,

I can't stop thinking

About that piece of my soul you took

My heart is so pure yet in such pain,
My God is so good,
He revealed MY failures,
So that OTHER women could gain.
Positive thoughts, time caught up
Compelled to reach back, grab a friend
Jealousy and hate make you let go again.
Innocence taken, through lies and deceit
I will never give up, go get it,
Yes that's me!
Different than any source you will ever meet,
You say I'm better off now, even made threats,
Watch my companies grow,
Yes I'm in flow
You are the last to take a piece of MY soul,
Narc,
This is something you better know,
Like your fake identity,
That will be checked
Make no mistake,
"I'm not there yet!

----DeAnne Michelle Rhynehardt-Bousso

"Still I Rise"

About The Author

My name is DeAnne Michelle Rhynehardt-Bousso. I am third, born of four kids in my family and named after my mother whose name is Pricilla Anne Rhynehardt. My mother was a single parent who sometimes worked three jobs to take care of her family; she overcame an abusive relationship, and she was also adopted at a young age. Sometimes, we had no electricity or gas in our home; she never gave up and never gave us away she just kept working. I grew up in Columbus, Ohio, whereby most people think it is a farm town; in some cases, it is I believe that the experiences my mother overcame made me who I am because she showed us nothing but love.

I was a girly girl as a young child with lots of ambition. I went to Ohio Dominican University where I majored in International Business and studied French at the University of Sorbonne, in Paris, France. I speak French as a second language to English. I have always felt the need to inspire or motivate people since I was a child. I have three children: Antonio, Jermaine, and Michelle Rhynehardt. I have experienced two marriages, been hurt with one, and devastated with the other. Today, I am stronger and wiser than I have been in my life. I will never stop the fight for success.

My immediate Family (True to me),

I have two sisters and one brother, Terry was my sister who was very smart and had no fear she passed away of breast cancer, but she was a fighter to the end. Terry was a tomboy and loved sports. She was born January 4, 1965. Shonnie, born April 26, 1963, is my oldest sister she is by far the prettiest in appearance without her illnesses, and ultimately has the most beautiful spirit inside and out, she has an innocence about her that is so authentic and so true that anyone would notice on the first meeting; her ex-husband was a fool for letting her go, she is a diamond. Shonnie my oldest sister also has many forms of cancer along with Lupus, but she is a survivor in every sense of the word. Anthony is my brother also a skin, cancer survivor, active, sweet, and very passive. Make no mistake his kindness is very deceiving; he is a beast if disrespected. Christopher born February 27, 1987, the baby boy is healthy as a bodybuilder and is still finding himself he is sweet and also a beast if disrespected. This is a little insight into my family dynamics.

Thank you from my heart & soul!

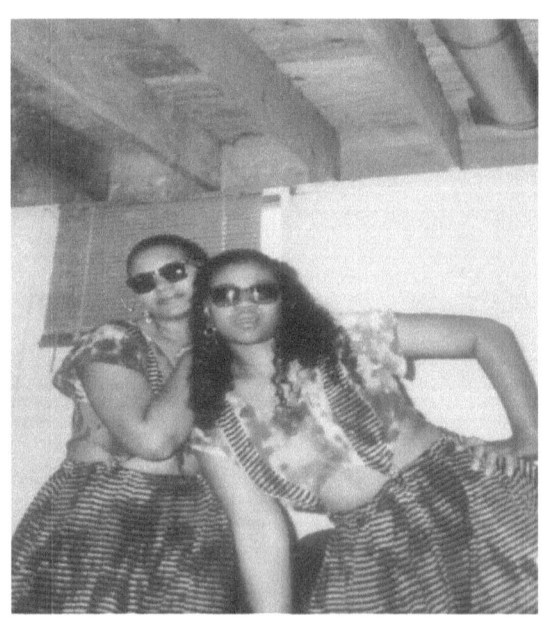

Dee & Lena

Family Matters

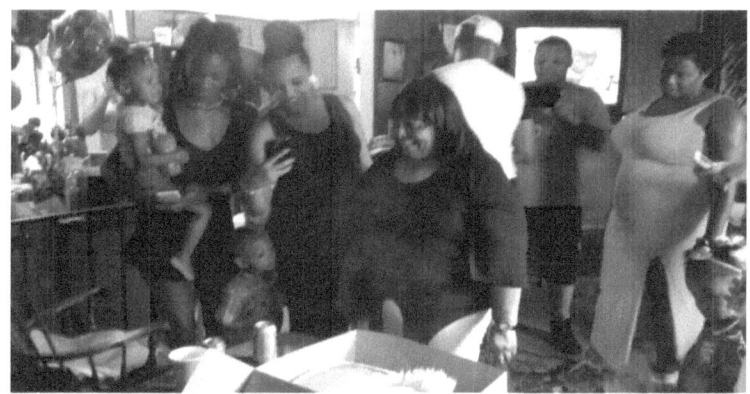

Family Fun

Terry & Tony

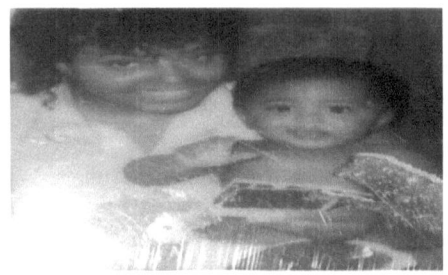

- family, is most important!

Other Books by this Author:

1. The Gift of Failing

2. Full Fledged

3. Success Is Not A Secret!

Goals 2018/2019

Resorces

Changes -in Your Life-

www.ingramcontent.com/pod-product-compliance
Lightning Source LLC
Chambersburg PA
CBHW031923240526
45464CB00022B/669